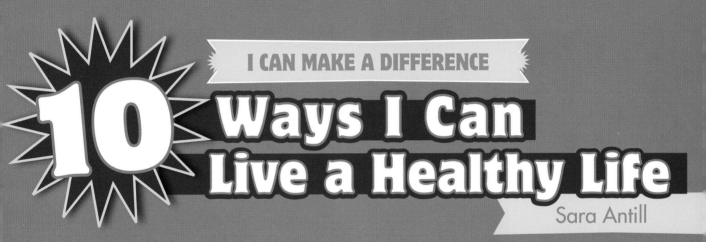

I CAN MAKE A DIFFERENCE

10 Ways I Can Live a Healthy Life

Sara Antill

D1205518

PowerKiDS press.

New York

To Cierra and Kaiya, two of my favorite girls!

Published in 2012 by The Rosen Publishing Group, Inc.
29 East 21st Street, New York, NY 10010

First Edition

Editor: Jennifer Way
Book Design: Ashley Drago

Photo Credits: Cover, p. 22 © www.iStockphoto.com/monkeybusinessimages; pp. 4, 8–9, 10 Shutterstock.com; p. 5 Lori Adamski Peek/Getty Images; pp. 6–7 © www.iStockphoto.com/Carmen Martínez Banús; p. 11 Stockbyte/Thinkstock; pp. 12–13 Thomas Northcut/Lifesize/Thinkstock; pp. 14–15 Jupiterimages/Comstock/Thinkstock; pp. 16–17 Jose Luis Pelaez/Getty Images; p. 18 iStockphoto/Thinkstock; p. 19 © www.iStockphoto.com/skynesher; pp. 20–21 Larry Bray/Getty Images.

Library of Congress Cataloging-in-Publication Data

Antill, Sara.
 10 ways I can live a healthy life / by Sara Antill. — 1st ed.
    p. cm. — (I can make a difference)
 Includes index.
 ISBN 978-1-4488-6207-8 (library binding) — ISBN 978-1-4488-6373-0 (pbk.) —
ISBN 978-1-4488-6374-7 (6-pack)
 1. Health—Juvenile literature. 2. Hygiene—Juvenile literature. 3. Nutrition—Juvenile literature.
4. Exercise—Juvenile literature. 5. Self-care, Health—Juvenile literature. I. Title. II. Title: Ten ways I can live a healthy life.
 RA776.5.A65 2012
 613—dc23
                                           2011033791

Manufactured in the United States of America

CPSIA Compliance Information: Batch #WW12PK: For Further Information contact Rosen Publishing, New York, New York at 1-800-237-9932

Contents

Healthy Living

Choosing to snack on fruit instead of sweets is one way to help keep your body healthy.

We make choices every day. Some of the most important choices we make are about how to take care of our bodies. Some things you do, such as eating fruits and vegetables, will help you grow strong and healthy. Other things can have harmful effects on your

health, though. It is important to take care of all the parts of your body.

Living a healthy life will help you feel good now, and it can also help your body stay healthy in the future. This book will show you 10 easy steps that you can take toward living a healthy life!

Exercising regularly and wearing protective gear when necessary are two choices that will keep you healthy and safe.

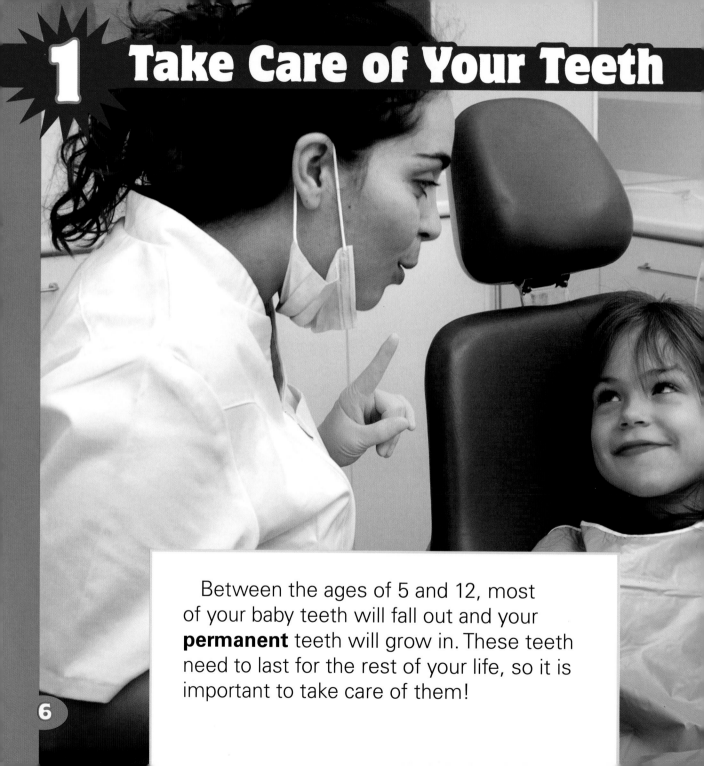

Between the ages of 5 and 12, most of your baby teeth will fall out and your **permanent** teeth will grow in. These teeth need to last for the rest of your life, so it is important to take care of them!

You need to brush your teeth twice a day. Be sure to brush the fronts and backs of all your teeth. Use floss to carefully clean the spaces between your teeth that a toothbrush cannot reach. Ask your parents to take you to the dentist twice a year. Your dentist will give your teeth a good cleaning and fix any problems, such as cavities!

Dentists give their patients advice on how to take good care of their teeth between visits. They can show you the best way to brush and floss your teeth.

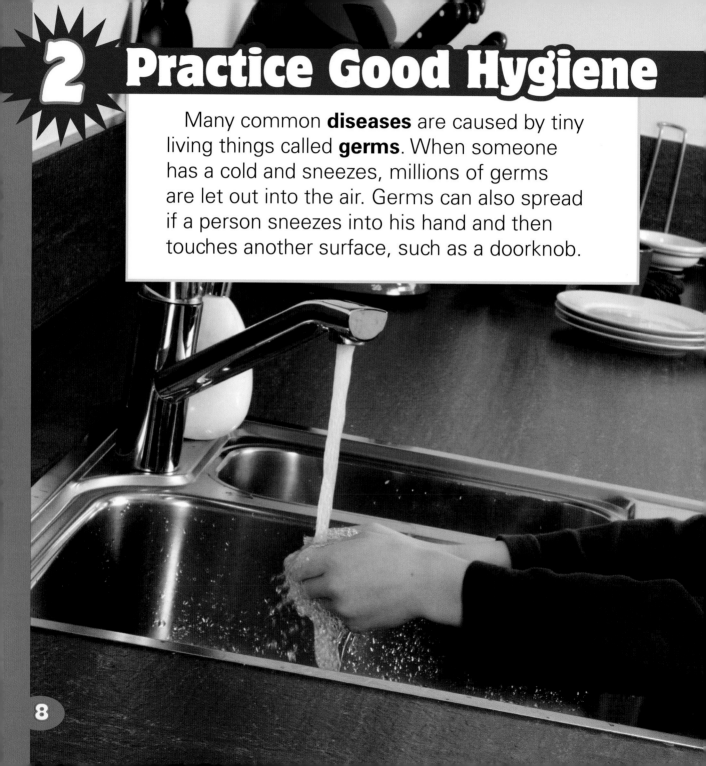

Many common **diseases** are caused by tiny living things called **germs**. When someone has a cold and sneezes, millions of germs are let out into the air. Germs can also spread if a person sneezes into his hand and then touches another surface, such as a doorknob.

When other people touch that surface, they can pick up those germs.

Good **hygiene** can help you stay healthy. Washing your hands often will wash off any germs that you have touched. You should also sneeze or cough into your elbow if you do not have a tissue. That way, you will not spread germs with your hands.

Washing your hands with soap and warm water cleans away germs. Regular soap does about as good a job of getting rid of germs as antibacterial soap.

3 Cut Out Junk Food

Apples are a good source of fiber, which is an important nutrient for your diet.

Some foods and drinks, such as candies and sodas, are often called junk foods. This is because they are low in **nutrients**. They are also often high in sugars and fats. Eating too much junk food can make your body sick. A healthy diet includes lots of fruits and vegetables and very little junk food!

4 Move Your Body!

Exercise is an important part of a healthy life. Look for opportunities to move your body instead of sitting down. See if you can walk or ride your bike to school instead of riding in a car or bus. You can even ask a friend who lives nearby to ride with you!

Riding a bicycle to school is a way to add more exercise to your life.

11

5 Learn a New Sport

Playing sports is a fun way to get more exercise in your life. Some sports, such as soccer and baseball, are played in teams. In other sports, such as tennis, one person plays against another person. In some sports,

such as golf and track, you may also be trying to top your own earlier scores or times instead of just trying to beat other people

You could play a sport at your school or see if your town has any sports **leagues** for kids. There may also be a cheerleading team or gymnastics class that you can join. Sports are a fun way to stay fit and to meet new friends.

Although there are lots of sports you can do at school or in a youth league, there are also sports and activities you can do with your family. This child is in a kind of boat called a kayak.

Many kids enjoy bike riding, rollerblading, and skateboarding. These are fun ways to exercise outdoors. It can be easy to fall and hurt yourself, though. Wearing a helmet and pads can help protect your body.

Most states have laws that say kids must wear bicycle helmets when they ride. These laws are to protect young riders. Helmets save riders' heads from serious harm about 85 percent of the time in a crash. Find a helmet that fits securely and comfortably on your head. Wearing knee and elbow pads can help protect you from scrapes, bruises, and broken bones.

Helmets are important safety gear for skateboarding, biking, and many other activities.

7 Protect Your Skin

Taking care of your skin is just as important as taking care of the rest of your body. Skin is strong and protects your body from harm. The Sun's rays can burn the skin, though. The harm caused by sunburns can lead to skin **cancer** later in life.

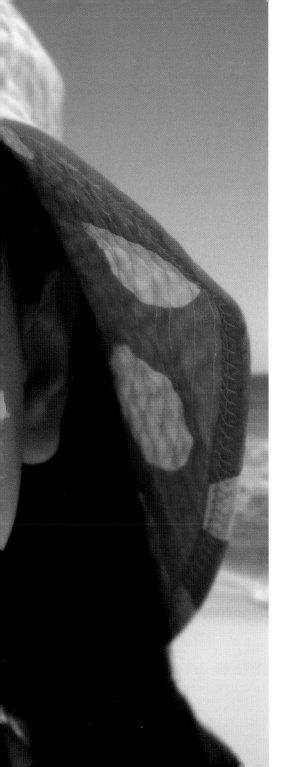

Sunscreen can help protect your skin from the Sun's rays. Sunscreens come with different Sun protection factors, or SPFs. Doctors say that all kids should wear sunscreen with an SPF of 30 or higher. Wearing long sleeves and a hat can also protect your skin. Protect your skin anytime you will be outside. You can even get sunburned on a cloudy day!

A wide-brimmed hat helps shade your face from the Sun. It is also important to reapply sunscreen throughout the day. You should use a sunscreen with a high SPF on areas that sunburn easily, like your cheeks and nose.

8 Get Enough Sleep

Lack of sleep makes it hard for you to concentrate at school. Over time, a lack of sleep can make you more vulnerable to catching colds or other illnesses.

Your brain is always working. When you are asleep, your brain sorts all the memories and information you took in during the day. When you do not get enough sleep, your brain cannot do this. Try to get between 8 and 10 hours of sleep every night. You will feel better and be able to think clearly at school.

9 Cut Down on Stress

Between school, activities, and friends, kids often have a lot of **stress**, or worries. Stress can cause stomachaches, headaches, and other problems. It can also make you less likely to do healthy things, like eating well. If you feel stressed, talk to a parent or friend. She may be able to help!

Many people find that doing yoga helps them let go of stress. Find out what relaxes you, and make that your go-to stress reliever.

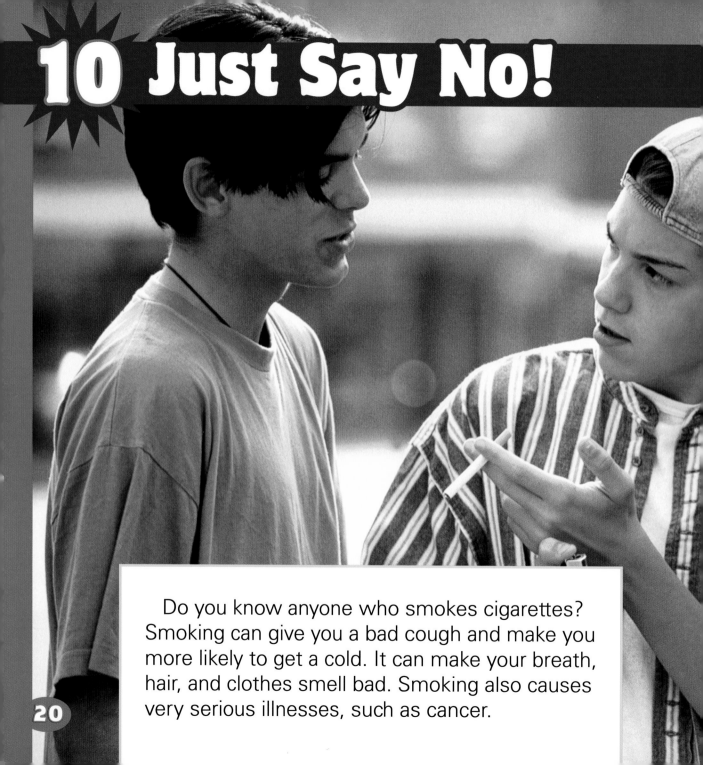

Do you know anyone who smokes cigarettes? Smoking can give you a bad cough and make you more likely to get a cold. It can make your breath, hair, and clothes smell bad. Smoking also causes very serious illnesses, such as cancer.

Cigarettes have a drug in them called **nicotine**. Nicotine is a very **addictive** drug, which means that once you start using it, your body will not want to stop. Smoking cigarettes for just a few days can get you addicted. Other drugs, such as cocaine and heroin, are illegal as well as addictive. Stay healthy by saying no to cigarettes and other drugs.

As with other drugs, smoking is an addictive, unhealthy habit. If someone offers you cigarettes or other drugs, just say no!

Help Others Stay Healthy

Living a healthy life is even easier when others around you are healthy as well. When lots of people share the same goal, they can encourage each other to do the things needed to reach that goal. Tell your family and the kids in your class about the ways you have learned to stay healthy.

Having a group of friends who all want to eat healthy and do healthy things makes it easier to do those things. See if you can get a group of friends from a team, from school, or from another group to join you in living a healthier life.

Starting a D.A.R.E. program in your school is a great way to teach other kids about the dangers of drugs. See if you and your parents can start riding your bikes around the neighborhood together on weekends. Being healthy can be a lot of fun!

Glossary

addictive (uh-DIK-tiv) Easily habit-forming.

cancer (KAN-ser) A sickness in which cells multiply out of control and do not work the way they should.

diseases (dih-ZEEZ-ez) Illnesses or sicknesses.

exercise (EK-ser-syz) Physical activity that is done to get or stay fit.

germs (JERMZ) Tiny living things that can cause sickness.

hygiene (HY-jeen) Practices that help you stay clean and healthy.

leagues (LEEGZ) Groups of sports teams.

nicotine (NIH-kuh-teen) A chemical found in tobacco.

nutrients (NOO-tree-ents) Food that a living thing needs to live and grow.

permanent (PER-muh-nint) Lasting for a long time.

stress (STREHS) Worries.

sunscreen (SUN-skreen) A cream that keeps the skin safe from the Sun's harmful rays.

Index

Web Sites

Due to the changing nature of Internet links, PowerKids Press has developed an online list of Web sites related to the subject of this book. This site is updated regularly. Please use this link to access the list: www.powerkidslinks.com/diff/health/